Doggy Biscuits

Poetic and Humorous Treats Inspired by the Billions of Dog Photos on my Phone

Doggy Biscuits

Poetic and Humorous Treats Inspired by the Billions of Dog Photos on my Phone

By Lizzie Nelson

Lizzie Nelson

Doggy Biscuits

ISBN (Print Edition): 979-8-9883723-0-1

For my husband
with apologies for all the times I said, "I love you"
and he said, "I love you too"
and I said, "I was talking to the dog."

And for Bixie, Sandie, Toby, Harvey,
and Charlie.

CONTENTS

INTRODUCTION

IN, WANTING OUT

OUTDOORS

INDOORS

LOOKS AND FEELS

DINNERTIME

AT THE END OF THE DAY

LITERARY, FILM AND TV CLASSICS

Introduction

FINDING LOVE

Hi. I'm Max. I'm German and I'm a Schnauzer. I like long walks in the... well anywhere. I like barking, squeaky-barking, getting under your feet, following you around, looking out the window, yawning in your face, food, my food, your food, goose and bunnypops (don't ask), movies with dogs in, smells, making smells, smelling my smells, cuddling and making smells. I hate rain, fireworks, and baths. I would like to meet... squirrels. We can take it nice and slow, don't feel you have to keep your distance though, I won't bite! Ha! Ha!

Hi, I'm Griffin and I'm a Schnorkie. You can call me Griff or my mum calls me Gruff, Treacle or Pony Ears. But I'm cool with anything you like, because ...

I'm a laid-back kind of guy. No lie.
I'm a laydeez man. Fact.
I am lady smack;
they all love this, you can touch this.
Half a pound of spice, I'm your Treacle,
I'll treat you nice, got moves of a weasel. Pop! Pop!
I'm nursery rhyming, fine dining, so fine I should be illegal.
I'm a napper, curl up on your lap uh!
I'm your rapper,
say my name, say my name,
ears of a pony, black and gold sweet pea,
everybody's baby.
Come and stroke me.

Hello, I'm Lizzie, Max and Griffin's Mummy. We became their proud parents in 2016, courtesy of Almost Home Schnauzer Rescue in Indiana. I soon began taking far too many photos, particularly when they came back from the groomers in fancy ties and bandanas, which I might rearrange for comic effect, take a photo and make up silly stories and poetry for social media.

Living in Chicago, the only other time they might have to get dressed up is when the weather is bitterly cold. Apart from that, they are normal rufty-tufty boys who have no idea that they are the butt of all my jokes, and I'd be grateful if you didn't tell them.

At the end of this book is a chapter of retold literary and film classics, each page alluding to a famous author, movie or series. No part is plagiarized, rather, just written in the rough style of each subject.

I hope this little book resonates with you and the love you have for the dogs that have been a rewarding part of your lives too.

I'm a sucker for beards
and big brown eyes,
between the two
I will not decide.
And so I live with my heart entangled,
with two hairy men in a love triangle.

In,
Wanting Out

ALL GROWN UP

If I were my own man
I'd be out not in
I'd be bad not good
I'd eat goose not food
I'd be loose not leashed
I'd be first not least
I'd be chaser not chaste
I'd be wolf not woof
I'd be riffraff not poofed
I'd be beast not boy
that is
until dinnertime.
Ok Mummy?

SUBURBIA WHEN YOU NEED A HAIRCUT

peoples
birds
eyebrows
bicycles
squirrels
FedEx man
DOGS!
children
eyebrows
cars
lawnmowers
leaf blowers
DOG!
mail-ladies
low cloud. No, sorry! Eyebrows.
Amazon trucks
eyebrows…

Looking Out the Window on a Sunny Day

What are you thinking beneath those brows?
The world outside
lights them up;
two too hairy callapitters
that birds and squirrels
and all breathing, living things arouse.
What are you thinking
under two busy, bushy brows?
Your eyes suck up creation
and you think the only thought
you ever have:
'I will catch that, and I will eat it up.
I will *schnauz*!'

Longing for the girl next door.
Longing for the leaves tossed along by the wind.
Longing for the worms left sun-dried and crispy on the path.
Longing for the little birds and fat squirrels.
Longing for the lamposts and trees and fire hydrants.
Longing for the smelly smells
and bunnypops and all manner of disgusting things in the grass.

LONGING FOR OUT

THE GIRL NEXT DOOR

Invisible fences around your heart.
Invisible fences keep us apart.
My princess in an electric tower,
our love is bound by unseen power.
Rapunzel, please take a step outside,
I promise you'll only get lightly fried.

THE GIRL NEXT DOOR ON A SNOWY DAY

Moira, Moira!
My girl next door ah
so adore ya!
But it's a freezah,
be sure your paws are
not stuck to the floor ya
haven't moved for
quite a bit, actually!

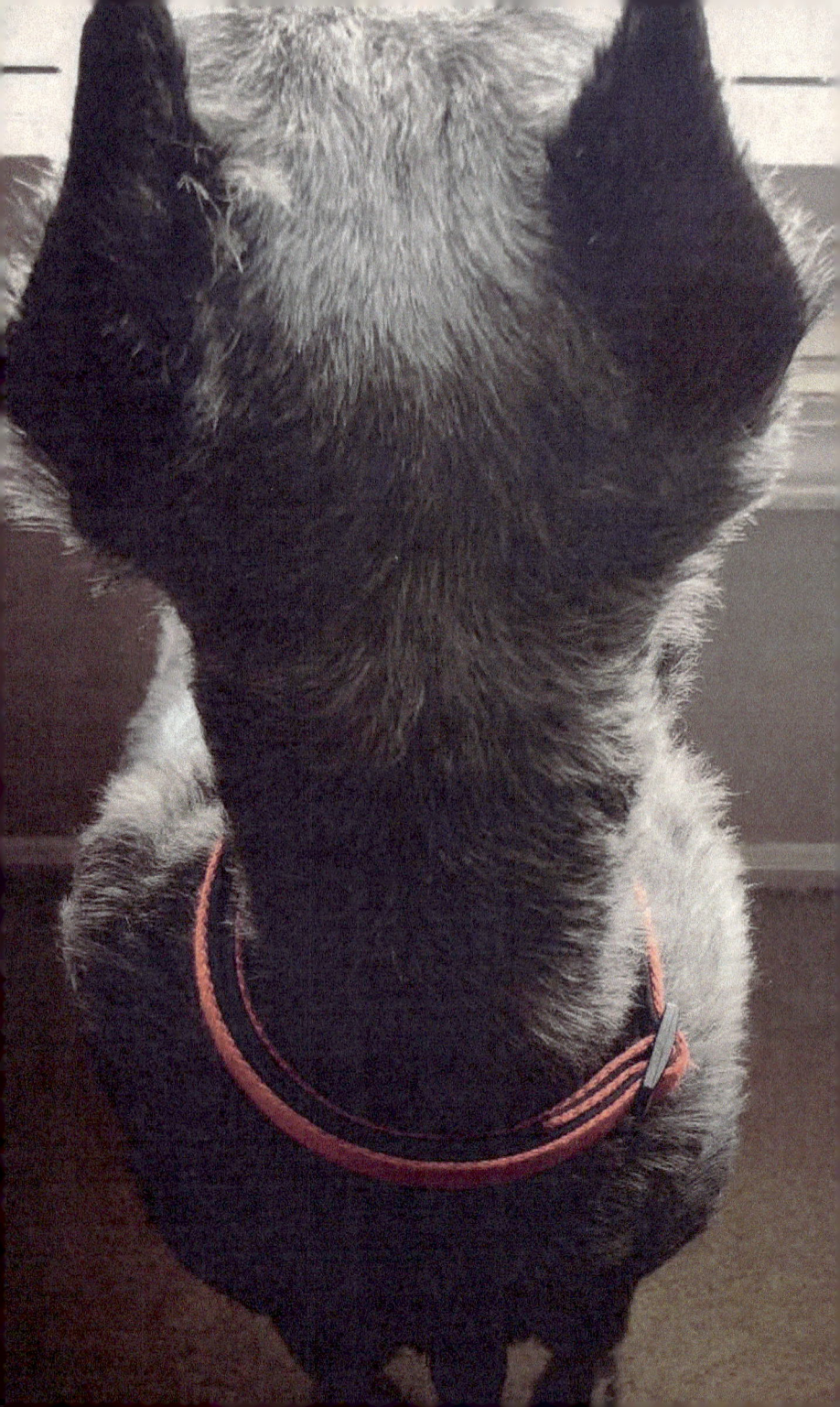

NEIGHBORHOOD WATCH

He is Neighborhood Watch,
a living search engine.
A skittle straight sentry,
antelope alert
with revolving radar ears.
If a bird so much as farts,
he sounds the alarm
with a bark as squeaky
as a smoke detector.
And we in turn, yell,
"Shut up you ruddy dog!"
Such is the cycle
of events in our house.
Every blasted day.

But we love him.

LOVE IN A TIME OF CORONA

I do not have the heart to say,
the girl next door has gone away.
His heart leaps when into view
walks any fluffy cockapoo,
then sinks again as none are Moira,
the girl he loved before err...Coroina.
Her family went on holiday
and now are stuck there, for who can say
how long these two are to be parted?
And so this boy is broken-hearted.

Baby Bunny I

You're just a tummy tickle,
like a canapé.
If you reprodushe,
my amuse-bouche,
I'll have a nice entrée!

Baby Bunny II

You are but a bitty bunny,
too tiny for my tum.
Although I'd love to eat you,
I'm more partial to your mum!

BUNNY

O furry thing with epic ears,
my need for you brings me to tears,
I love and hate you all the same,
so near, so far; it fries my brain.
You look so licky, all teasing twitches,
my heart, my nose, for you it itches!
Just promise me this before you flee;
leave bunnypops for Griffin and me.
They're our fav'rite!

SQUATCHING

I'm squirrel watching.
I'm watching you and
those buxom cheeks
filled by twitchy nibbles.
Then frozen features as you pause
to look right at me
trapped and double-glazed,
impotent indoors.
And I wince a little,
as you return to your meal
with another bite
from your nimbly nut-grasping paws.

Outdoors

Diligence

Dog
Log;
Bagged
Wagged

Dog
Plop;
Scooped
Poop

Dog
Squirt;
errr! ...
Let's pretend I didn't see that one!

Snow Patrol

I wish I was a Husky
living in the snow,
I'd be the leader of the pack
an' tell 'em where to go.

We'd go bark at bears an' narwhals
an' chase the snow patrol,
then to be extra speshl naughty,
we'd all pee on the South Pole.

PARK SONG (TO THE TUNE OF 'LET'S GO FLY A KITE')

Let's go to the park
where we can bark and bark!
Make Mummy wish the ground would swallow her
up and
look! There's a tiny child,
let's go all bonkers-wild
and lunge, all slavering,
like we will eat him
    and see!   A fake playground
                tree, the grandest place for us to pee;
        let's drag her over here (but make it look like it's
                                            her idea)
                and wow! There's a patch of ice,
                    to tear across it would be nice.
                    Not to worry, she's still upright
                    and moving at the speed of light!

BARK! BARK! Wait! That looks yum.
Spit that out? Do we have to, Mum?!
The bunnies left them here for us;
little popsies in the grass.
And whoa Lady! Is that your pup?
So tiny! And why's he all dressed up?
Don't hold him up so high
   beyond our leap; he's terrified!
                    And BARK!! BARK! Oh lovely day!
                         Pretty birds don't fly away!
                    Wingy things all directions fled;
             our leashes twist round Mummy's legs
             and oh! She's flipped onto the ground
                to get kisses from her happy hounds.
             Dearest Lady, we know you long to be
                       united with a cup of tea.
                   Maybe something stronger still!
                           Let's get you home.
                              Wait…OH BOY!

SQUIRREL!!!

MAX HAS A THOUGHT

When I spot a dog
across the street,
we have a bit of a verbal argy-bargy,
then I do a really serious pee on the nearest thing,
which says, 'I have a reserve tank,
I am superior.
This side of the road is mine.'

When Griffin spots a dog
across the street,
he don't say much but bristles up to twice his size,
then does a serious pee on the nearest thing
and kicks up the grass, real good,
which says, 'I have a reserve tank,
I am superior.
This side of the road is mine.'

When Mummy sees another mummy
across the street,
they have a bit of a chat
then... I know she wants to
but she holds it in 'til she gets home.
Just.

SAME TIME TOMORROW?

Here comes that lamppost where you have to pee
and that hydrant and that tree.
Here's the house with the Pyrenees
you love but can't reach past her knees.
Here we sniff where the squirrel sat.
There we roll where the bunnies crapp'd.
And me,
picking up everything after you
because every day
is déjà poo.

BUMBLEBEE

O fuzzy Schnauzies on the wing;
my favorite part of every Spring,
to watch them buzz the primroses
with nectar on their little noses.
I really, really cannot wait
to see Max go out and pollinate!

ROLLING

Something stinky in the grass,
too lovely just to snuffle past!
My mummy watches me aghast
as I roll and rub it head to arse!

ODE TO AUTUMN

Season of wet paws in the early morning.
Season of stupid prickle balls in my beard.
Season of barking at small shrill things on their way to
school.
Season of cobwebs in the grass
and tickly tasting spiders in the house.
Season of squirrel-scented nut-casings raining from the
trees
and littering the paths.
Season of dumb-ass squirrels taunting me and scuttling
along fences and up the trees as we pass.
Season of squirrels splattered wafer thin on the roads,
season of...you know what?
I bloody love Autumn!

After Robert Frost

Whose pup this is I think I know.
His mummy's in the village, though;
She will not mind me stopping here
To watch his brows fill up with snow.

AFTER ROBERT HERRICK

Whenas in sunshine my Griffin goes,
There's nothing more lovely, I do suppose
Than the sweet perfection of his nose.

When I cast mine eyes, and see
That wee wet button lit, adorably
O how that glittering taketh me!

Indoors

EAVESDROPPING

"Imagine if they were part Schnauzies;
all our friends, in all these housies!
Penny and Lucy, aren't they Cockers?
They'd make a lovely pair of Schockers!"
"Terry Teacup, if he were Schnauzer,
might become a little Trouzer."
"Or that American Poodle that fancies you,
she would make a great Schampoo!"
"And don't forget that sweet Ridgeback,
she could be a tasty Schnack!"
"And Pixie's half a Pekinese
(and gives her mum the allergies),
so she'd become a little *Schneeze!*"

THE SCHCARLET PUPPERNEL

I see him here!
I see him there!
I see that beefcake everywhere!
Is he real?
He seems so misty,
that demned elusive sexy beastie!

Throwback Thursday

Throw it!
Watch me snatch it
I will catch it
in my chops.

Pitch it!
Watch me chip it
Golden Snitch it
as it drops.

Just chuck it.
See me chomp it
if you launch it.

Throw it.
Throw i…
Crap!
Throw it again!

LICKY

Ew! There's a wet patch on my sofa, Max.
From which end did it come?
Or was it both ends at the very same time
because you licked your BUM!

DOGGY BISCUITS

thank you for my doggy biscuit
where oh where is best to eat it?
I must take it to a carpet
where it will shatter when I bite it
as nothing hacks off Mummy more
than licking crumbs off rugs
and not bare floor!

You're Not Bringing That Indoors!

Altho I haf found this luvly fevver,
I am a poor forlornly fella,
for she won't let this clever dog
chew it on her fancy rug.

I've tried to sneak in bunny pops
and clods of fur the foxes dropped
but she shrieks and puts on rubber glubs
and bins everyfink I found and lubs.

I've told her I will run away,
and live where I'll be ME all day;
eating fings she'd say were ick,
until I do a mammoth sick.
And then you know what I will do?
I'll jolly well eat that up too!

TREASURE HUNTER

All the good stuff has gone under the sofa!
I can't paw out the plunder!
Mummy, please
come and look.
Yes! Get the broomstick.
That's it!
On your hands and knees.
Please stop swearing!
Hurry up!
I promise not to stick my nose
on your builder's bum.

CATCH ME IF YOU CAN

If joy was
as easy as
seizing a toy
in your cheeky chops.
If laughter came
as peasy as
teasingly
offering it to me
only to run away
and giggle under a chair.
And if kindness was
as lemon squeezy as
offering the
soggy end
for me to chew,
I say let's play!
And ...
catch me if you can!

Irresist

Tickle me, Mummy
Tickle my tummy
Tickle me here
Tickle me there
Tickle me where there is no hair
Tickle me silly - I don't even care.
My tickle pose melts you, I know, deep inside
And gives YOU tummy tickles
When you look in my eyes!

Stair Warmers

Pre-warmed stairs are such a treat,
lovely for unslippered feet.
But I've only two, so I need more
dogs for heating up my floor.
Let's give the local shelter a call,
count the steps from landing to hall.
RING RING
"Yes, we need eleven more dogs, straight away, please!
With big fluffy bums, so our feet don't freeze!"

NOWHERE MAN

The torpid hours.
I am but a waif
flickering
in the half-life
on the edge of existence.
That agonizing limbo,
stretching eternal,
between walkies
and dinnydins.

EAVESDROPPING II

"That is one beautiful day!"

"The way the sun hits the green and dazzles your eyes!"

"And the knowledge that everything's doing what it's meant to do: birds flying,
plants photosynthesizing, animals foraging…"

"The perpetual rhythm of life, we're all on a preordained path."

"True, but I'm more of an existentialist myself."

"Oh wow, err… me too. When did she last clean these windows?"

"I know, right? I did that nose print in 2016."

"Disgusting! She should wipe it off."

"No, it's art; it represents my existence on the physical pane."

"BRUH!"

Looks
and Feels

BAT IN THE CAVE

Why don't dogs get bogeys?
Max wondered if I knows.
I don't have the answer
but there's something up your nose.

If dogs do not get bogeys,
then what crawled *in* your snout?
Cos that is more disturbing
than something coming out.

Collar

Click unclipped
Oh, how I need to lick it,
is it…
what is it?
Love it, hate it.
I'm conflicted.
A bit of me
I never see,
that comes off in your hand,
that band.
And
is it friend?
Where you and I
begin and end?
This part of me
that detaches.
This part of you
that matches us and says,
you're my lady
and
I'm your baby.

THE AIR BETWEEN US

When we're so close
that I can bury my face
in the warmth of your neck
and have my arms around you
running up and down your back.
And when your ear is pressed against my cheek
and I feel a well of love rising,
filling my universe.
When I hear you sigh,
deflating in contented repose
and you pull back your head to shyly
catch my eye,
why must you
always blinking
sneeze in my face?!

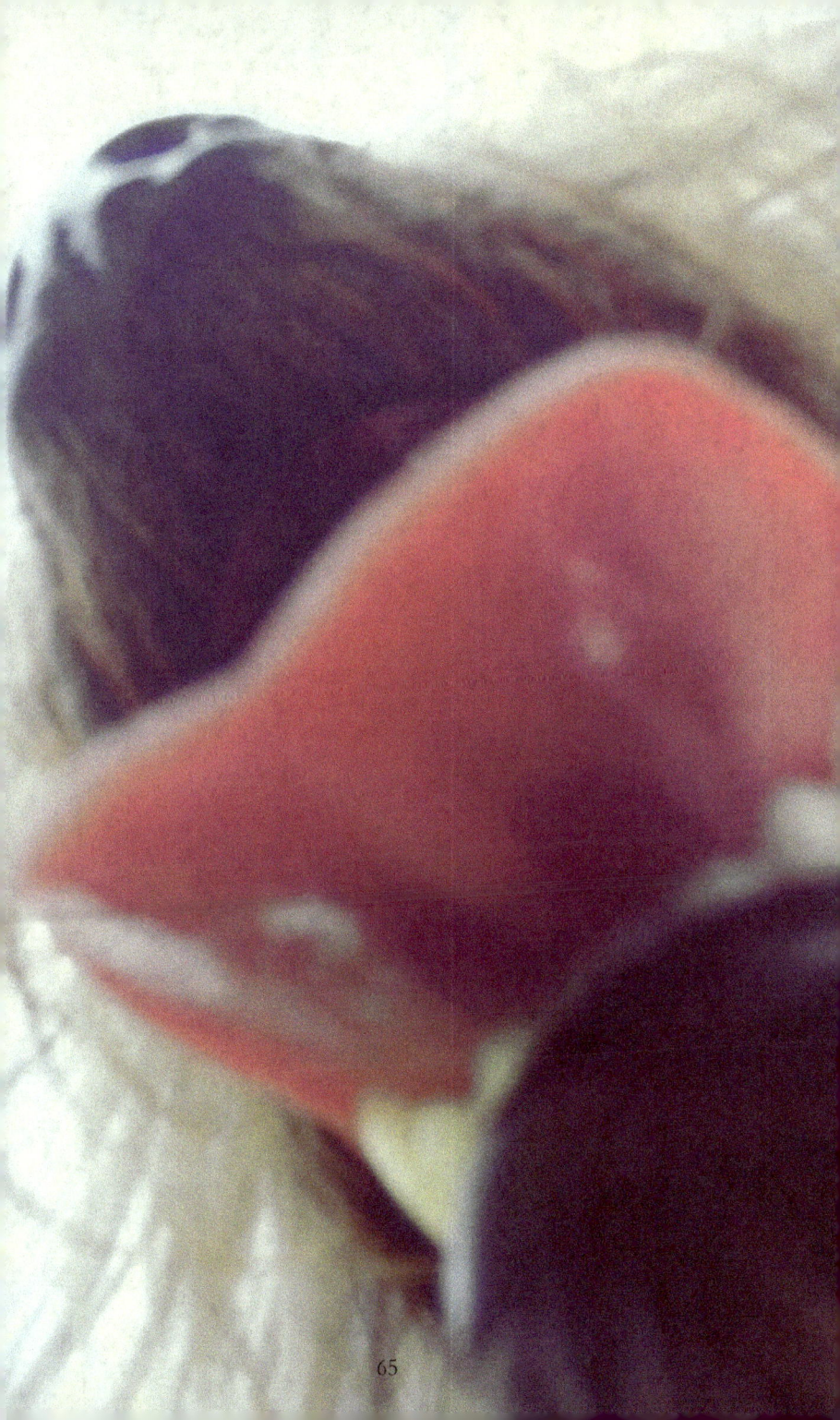

SWORL

There is a whorl on your neck
like a tiny eddy spinning in a river of fur.
Or a spiral galaxy
that I can stick my little finger in.

BEARD

Gentle breezes waffle it
Ladies softly fondle it
Men envy the swell and billow of it
Squirrels fear and worship it
and Mummy says I'd look like Gonzo without it.

HOME GROOMING IN A TIME OF CORONA

They left my eyebrows and beard on the floor,
clipped the fluff off my bum and my paws.
I squeaked when they snipped at my todge
and I swore.
But look at me now, I mean,
PHWOAR!!

VET

Two little boys are restless,
Griffin and his chum.
It pays to be suspicious
in a place that pokes yer bum.

Two little boys are whimpering,
I know they know what's up.
But in comes a lady who seems awfully nice
with treats for both my pups.

Two little boys are quivering,
their tummies tied in knots,
as there echoes that nurse's parting words;
"She'll be right in with your shots!"

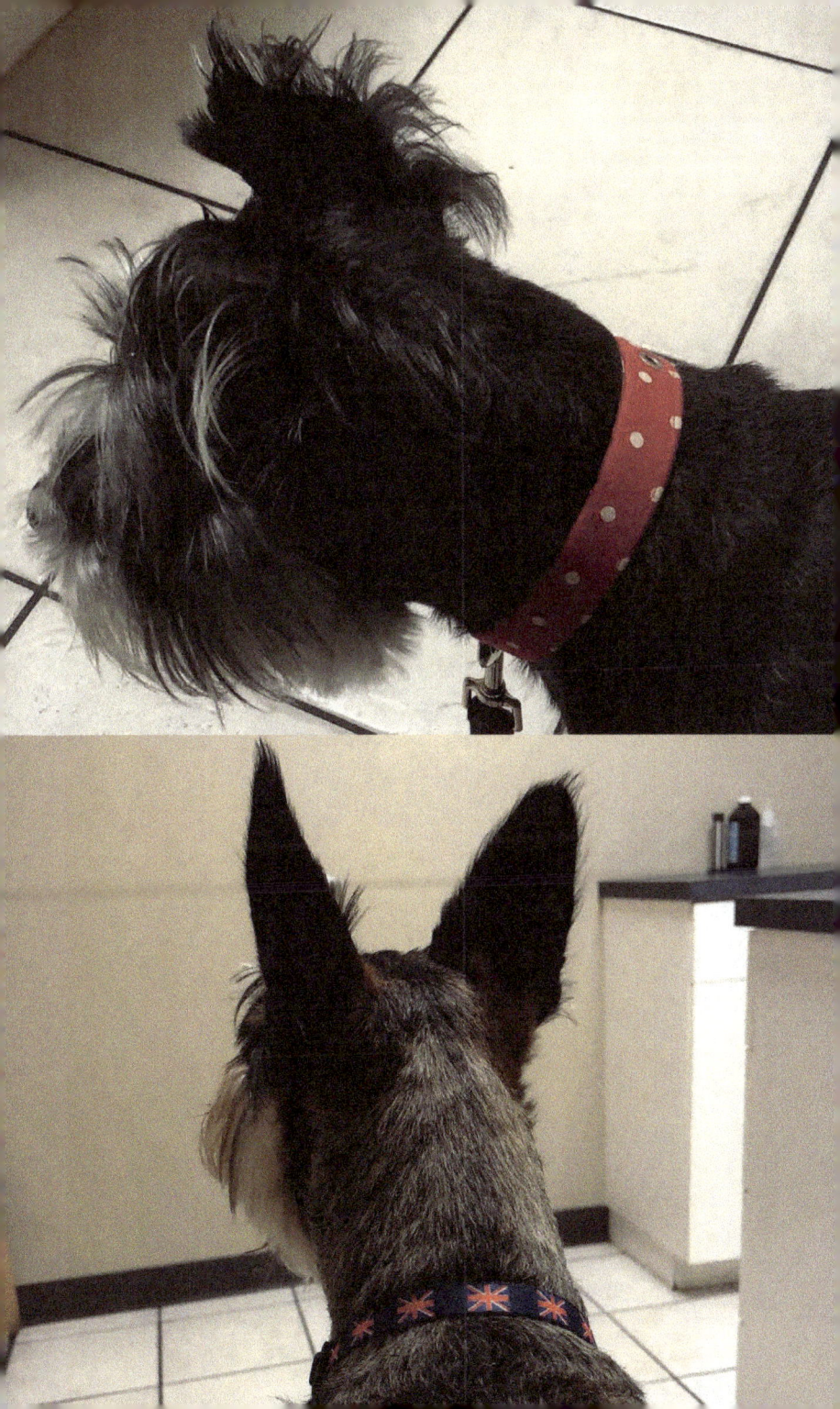

NOSIES

When you proposes
don't buy me red roses
a bunch of wet noses
is better by far.
One might get lonely,
two's just okay, but
only a dozen wet noses
will win you my heart.

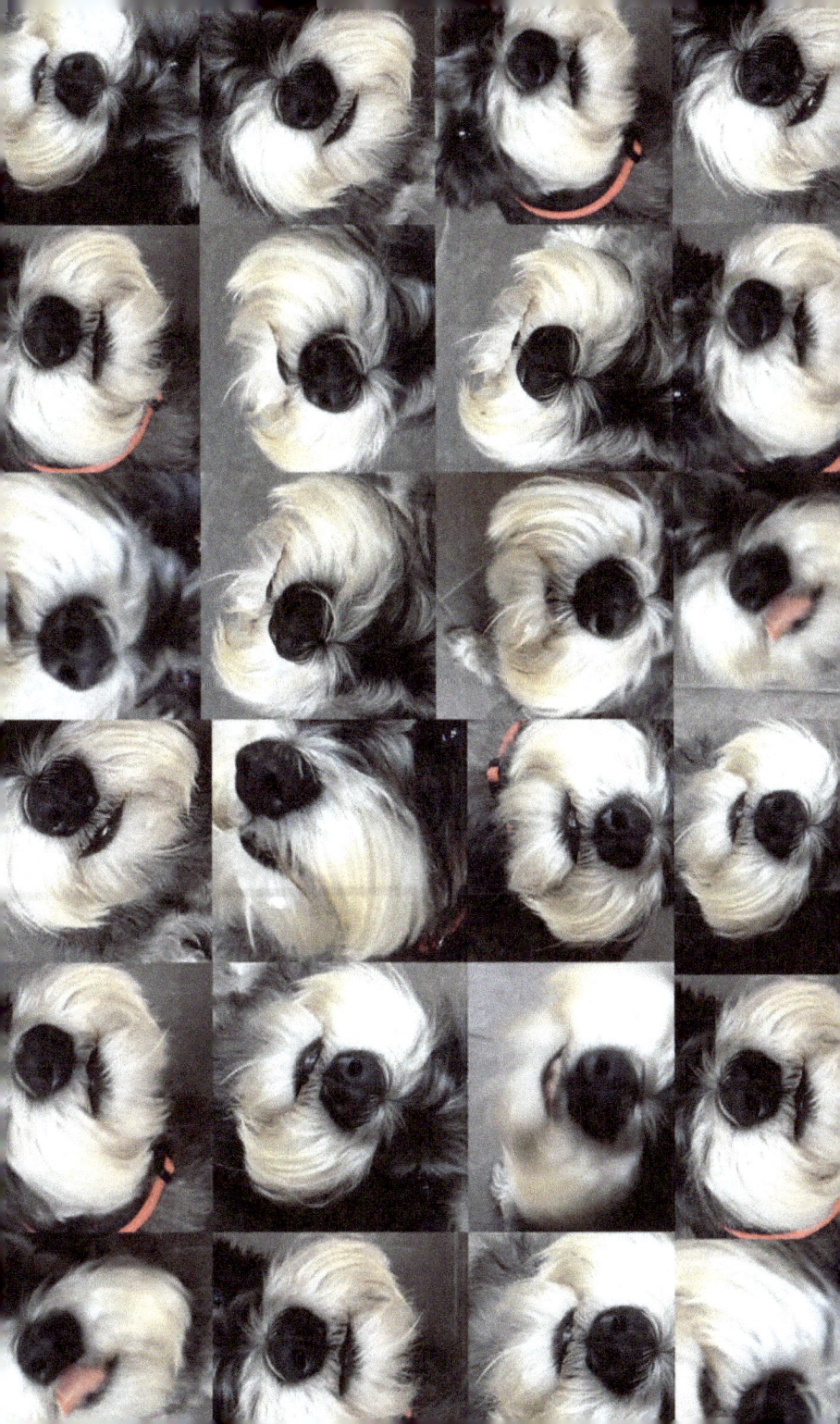

PUFFS

Imagine if, like dandelion seeds,
your eyebrows caught the balmy breeze
and floated over sea and sand
to settle in some far-flung land.
And there to grow and blanket meadows,
blousy bobbing downy echoes
of my bonny boy.

COMMUNICATION

It's a beautiful thing.
I mean, who needs words?
We have conversations by look and touch, by gesture.
The language of love and friendship, and trust.
Unsaid, wordless, and still
such deep understanding.

Oi! Who did that?
Why didn't you say you needed a poo?!

BONDED

I am the dog that is under your feet,
one pace behind you
when you're up from your seat.
I am the chap that stands on the rug
you are trying to straighten,
yes, I am that dug.
I am the pup that will walk on your chest
when you're blissfully napping,
free of all stress.
I am the child that takes twenty minutes to poo
for it must be quite perfect when your mum's frozen
through.
I am the boy that makes smells when we snuggle,
whose botty always
gets me in trouble.
So perfect a Mummy
is why I'm devoted to you.

(But just so you know,
I smell your smells too!)

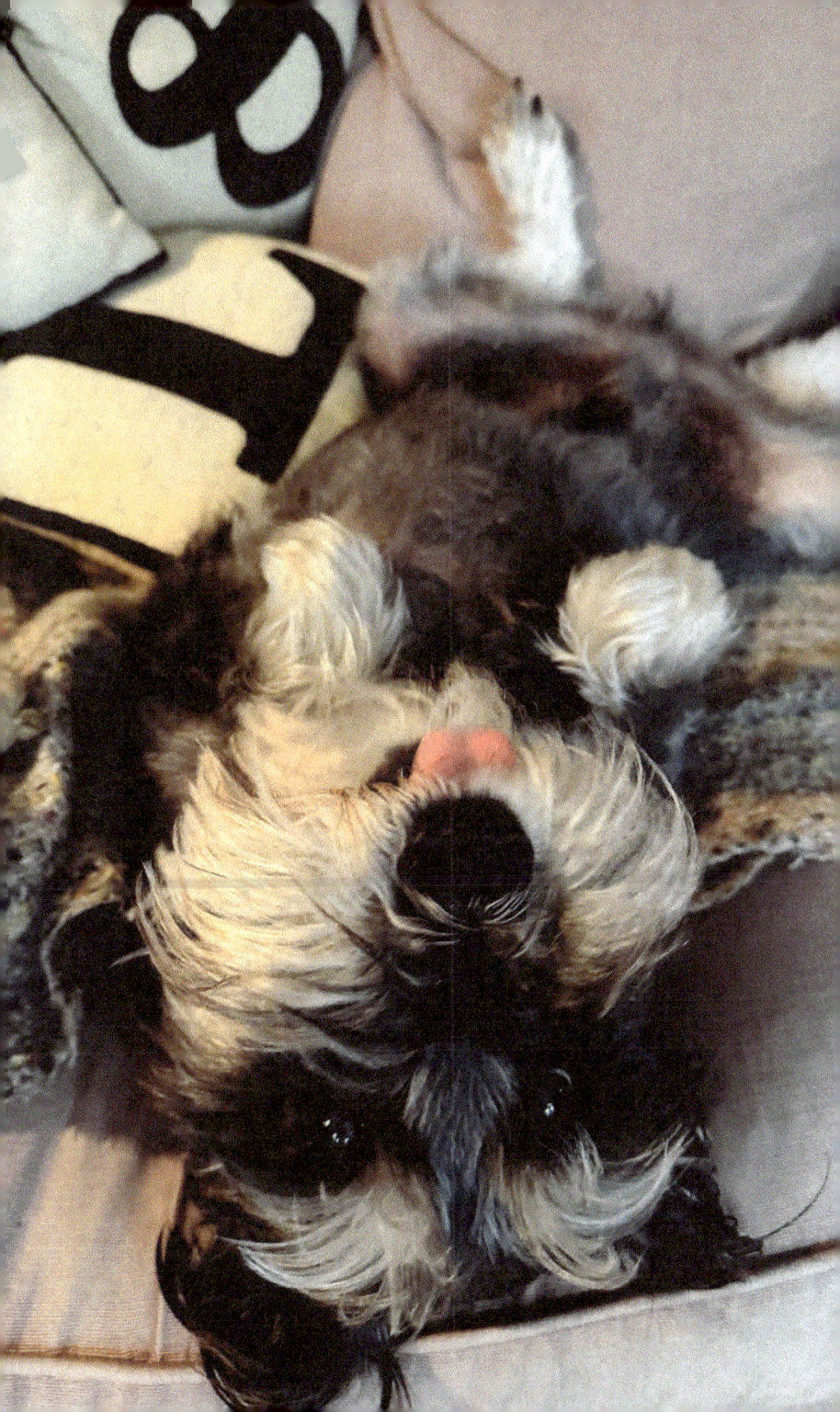

Dinnertime

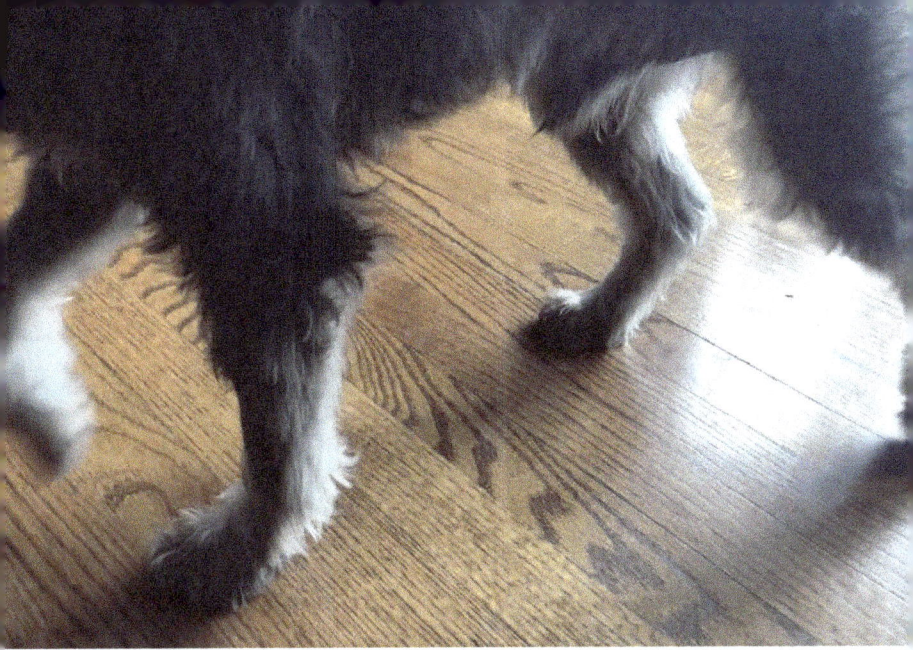

TOENAILS

Tikka takka, tikka takka, tikka takka, tik
        kit, akkat akkit, akkat akkit, akkat akkiT

Tikka takka, tikka takka, tikka takka, tik
        kit, akkat akkit, akkat akkit, akkat akkiT

Tikka takka, ti… OK MAX! Stop pacing! I'll get your dinner!

SIX O'CLOCK PRIORITIES

Mummy, it's dinnertime!

Mummy! I love you. And it's dinnertime!

Mummy, Mummy, Mummy, you're so lovely.... And it's dinnertime!

Mummy! Look into my eyes... din-ner!

Mummy, I'm fading away!

Mummee! I'm slipping into unconsciousness. Need food.

Can't hold on. You're getting blurry!

C'mon! It's 6 o'clock; it's your favorite time of day, my Mummy!

Yes! That's it! Up you get!

Wait! What?!

You're fixing yourself a DRINK?!

TUMMY CLOCKS

Our tummy clocks were ticking
when clinking bowls were heard,
we stopped what we were doing (which was bugger all)
and came as quick as birds.
So hurry up and pick a tin,
we don't care much what's in it.
Just hurry up with dinny-dins,
we can't wait another minute!
Why must it take so bloody long?
Please concentrate and get it done.
See our pleading faces, Mum;
our twinkly eyes, our wagging bums.
Yay! Our eyes connect,
you leave your zone
and reach for what?!
Your blinking phone?!
Don't take our pho.. no! Goddam!
This is NOT the time for Instagram!

So Unfair!

When I'm watching you eat,
do you know what I'm really thinking?
I eat at 9.
I eat at 6.
You eat at 8, 9, 10.30, 10.34, 11.15,
12, 1.04, 2, 5, 6.11, 6.20, 7 and 8.45.
This is not my begging face,
it's my,
'What the actual floof, Woman!?' Face.

Maxapology

It's not in my nature
to be a thief,
but if Griffin
ain't quick to eat his treats,
well,
my brain works way after my teef!

Counting Calories

That's the fifteenth snack you've snacked today,
our Mummy,
please share with us that final bite.
That's it! Two bits left, you gorgeous lady,
just… Oi!
No wonder you've got cellulite!

At the End of the Day

SCHNOOZING

Afternoon schnoozles on my knee.

Two lazy bums dribbling on me.

One does a fart like old blue cheese

...smells quite nice, actually!

Clocking Off

Your work is done for the day.
There are no more Amazon trucks pulling up,
no more mowers and blowers outside.
No rustle of wrappers, clink of bowls
or plink of crumbs
dropping to the kitchen floor.
No kid bursting in from school,
tossing her backpack and kicking off shoes
to cuddle you on the stairs.
No Daddy turning his key
in the front door.
For all your people are home and safe.
So come and join us,
on the sofa,
and we'll watch Yellowstone together.

Wait! Are you snoring?!

COUNTING

Go to sleep, go to sleep,
count those bunnies in Dreamland.
Oh you missed one!
Better catch him
and pop him in your tum!
Go to sleep, Little Boy,
your Mummy is watching.
Go to sleep, Tiny Pup,
she will keep you from harm.

But actually, could you spit that last one out, he was
rather cute.

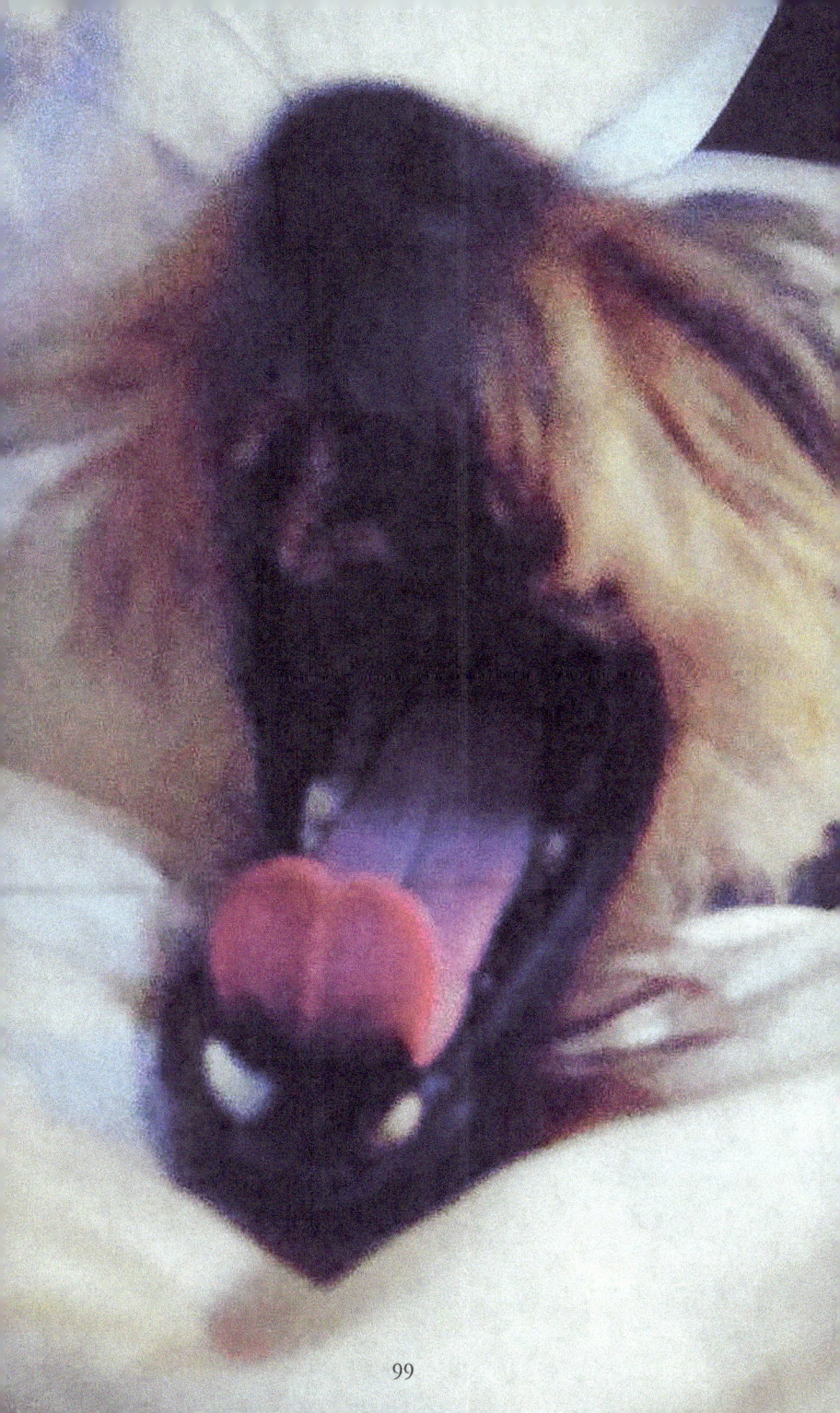

SCHNAPPING

Rest your chin, little chap, on my lap.
Lick your chops, close your eyes, take a nap.
It's been a helluva day;
so much yapping and play
and icky things
lovingly lapped.

WISHES

May the morning bring a big boy's beard
and all the squirrels be afeared.
So brave and bristly you will be,
they'll scamper up the tallest tree
(except that ginormous one you'll catch for tea!).

CALCULATIONS

They count our love by strokes.
They judge affection by the cheese we share.
They gauge acceptance by not being kicked off our bed.
They weigh commitment by walks
and devotion by dinner on time.
But what they have given to us
is immeasurable.

Geroff!

It's not the morning sun that filters through my window.
It's not the woodpecker in the woods across the way.
It's not the anticipation of my first cup of coffee,
making promises for a fruitful day.
It's not the gentle purr of a CPAP
or my bladder pushing sleep away.
No.
You know what wakes me every bloody morning?

But I wouldn't have it any other way.

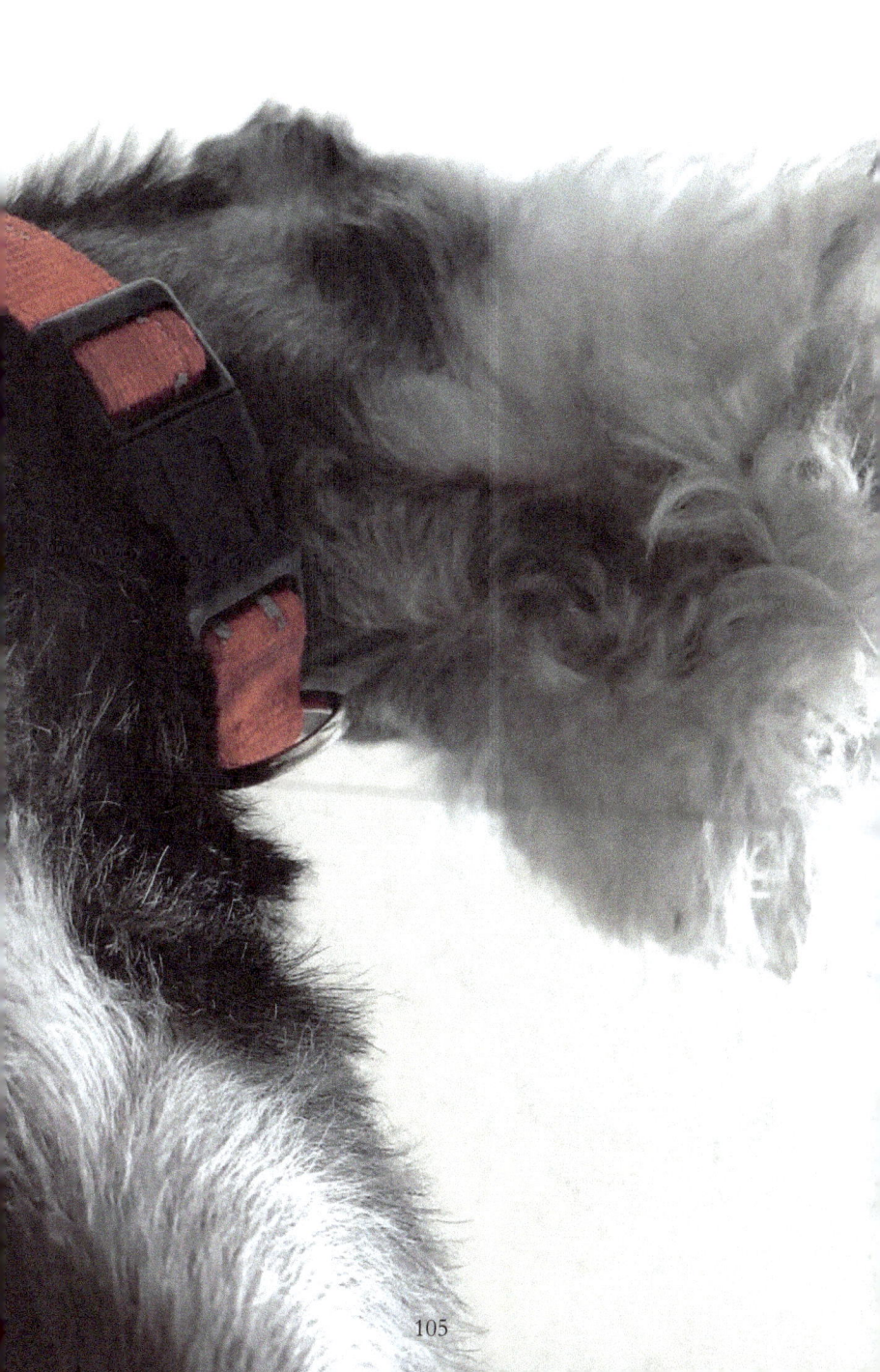

He Hunts in Dreams

When he twitches in his sleep, I know,
he hunts in dreams.
He flies through woods in pursuit of dragons.
When he yips, I know,
he debates Parliament,
plots coups and commands armies.
When he chatters, I know,
he's probably doing a press conference.
In his dreams, he wins landslide elections,
has dominion over the world.

And then he wakes up and sees us,
I know, with a look of mild disdain.

CRADLE SONG

Sleep, sleep,
Sweet Pupperino.
Sleep, sleep,
brown-eyed boy.

Your twitchy slumber makes me wonder,
in your Dreamland, do you fly?
Are you chasing all the birdies;
hunting geese across the sky?
Are you hovering in the treetops?
And do the squirrels scream?
Dropping all their nuts in horror,
oh, what a lovely dream!

Sleep, sleep,
Sweet Puppletto.
Sleep, sleep,
my brown-eyed boy.

The New Girl Next Door

Tonight, I'm going to dream of Shirley, Mummy,
I'm going to chase her round the yard!
Then she'll chase me
and I'll chase her
and she'll chase me
then I'll collapse on the daisies, panting,
and she'll run over and roll in the grass
and I'll roll in the grass
and she'll roll in the grass
and while I'm catching my breath
she'll leap up,
all pouncy and bouncy on those long, long legs,
and bark at me
then I'll bark at her
then we'll bark at the birds
then bark at nothing in particular
then she'll chase me
and I'll chase her
and...Oh Mummy! I think I love her!

But she's absolutely exhausting!

Thanks Lady

Because of you
I have a bed.
Because of you
I'm warm and fed.
You stroke the worries from my head
and tuck me in to catch my zeds.
I don't do words,
so it goes unsaid,
but let me lick your face instead.

And just when you thought it was all over, Max and Griffin retell some

Literary, Film and TV Classics

Sir Arthur Conan Doyle: Sherlock Holmes

It was nearly June, but Sherlock and Watson still wore overcoats as they stepped out into the chilly wet morn.
"Why's that then, Sherlock?"
"Climate change, innit, my dear Watson!"
"But why do we have to look like a couple of wallies?"
"That's elementary, Old Boy; Mummy went to TK Maxx!"

Stephenie Meyer: The Twilight Saga

Although she was repeatedly warned to lock herself in her room, Bella knew that Jacob would not harm her once he transformed. But nothing prepared her for the size of his gnashers and revolting dog breath.

Catherine Cookson: Tilly Trotter

"And Tilly, when you've finished with the washing and dusting, you can make me a nice cup of tea! Oh, and don't forget to scrub the doorstep; we can't have the neighbors thinking we're not respectable!"

Mark Twain: The Adventures of Huckleberry Finn

Huck and Tom could not wait to hit the open road. Huck knew it was wise to take provisions for the journey. The nights on the river could be lonely and so silent, well apart from the cicadas and the singin' of the frogs 'n' toads, the 'gators and the nightingales, the coyotes and the owls, the endless buzz of 'squitoes, the music and laughter from the paddle steamers and the eerie tones of harmonicas drifting from Lord knows where. Yup! Best take Lil' Ted with 'em, then they wouldn't be afeared of nuthin!

Jack London: The Call of the Wild

I knew Buck hated me for putting him in the full Arctic kit before harnessing him, but for his own good, I ignored the look of contempt in his eyes. The other sled dogs would laugh at him, I knew, but his little red booties would ensure he didn't lose another unfortunate appendage to frostbite.

H.G. Wells: The Invisible Man

Although last night's experiment had failed, he felt the power was so nearly within his grasp, it would just take enormous concentration. However, when he needed it most, at a moment of absolute crisis when Mummy had decided that they needed a bath and he was next to go in, despite trying with all his might, Griffin could not turn invisible.

Tracy Chevalier: Girl with a Pearl Earring

Lotte had never sat for a portrait before, but the artist had seen something in her, an innocence and strength born out of a childhood plugging dykes around her father's clog farm. She sat for him in traditional dress, but he had insisted she wore her mistress's pearl earrings. She prayed that nobody would notice that she had accidentally eaten one.

Frances Hodgson Burnett: The Secret Garden

October 7, 1898. Little Lord Fauntleroy (right) and the gardener's son, Dickon (left) had been playing in the secret garden all day. Nanny was exceedingly cross with the state of them as they burst excitedly into the nursery. She promptly scrubbed them with carbolic soap and made them put on fresh 'kerchiefs. They were then to sit and wait, as quiet as nuns, in the Master's study until his return.

Little did they know the Master was not to return until 1902 and the conclusion of the Boer War.

Francis Hodgson Burnett: A Little Princess

Maxine could not understand why all the other children were given baby squirrels for tea and she got nothing. Licking the floors clean was now her only sustenance. Miss Minchin explained that her father had not been sending money to the school for several weeks. She should prepare herself for the fact that her only parent was probably lost in the Amazon …Distribution Center.

Anne Brontë: The Tenant of Wildfell Hall

Acclimatizing to life in a small Yorkshire rural society was hard. Not that they weren't kind, godly people but Helen found it terribly challenging to put aside their lack of manners. At the Hargraves' dinner party, the Squire ate with his mouth open throughout the entire meal. She honestly thought she might faint with the horror of it.

E.M. Forster: Howard's End

Lucy and Cecily were waiting for afternoon tea on the terrace. It had been a particularly taxing day and even a little troubling. Howard, their gardener, had been tickling Cecily in the rose garden when a telegram had come informing them that their uncle, the Admiral, had been lost at sea.

A troubling end to a delightful summer's day, but nothing that a cup of Darjeeling and a dog biscuit wouldn't fix.

Cecily comforted herself licking the crumbs from her saucer as she idly watched Howard's end as he dug up the potatoes for dinner.

Dan Brown: The Da Vinci Code

Dr Langdon knew it was more than just a dog biscuit. Sure, embossed across the top was the word 'Bonio' but the underside had curious textured markings. He nibbled it cautiously, aware that the Rotary Club could be watching from the shadows. Alas, before he realized his mistake, he had eaten the whole thing and with it any hope of saving the world.

E. L. James: The Fifty Shades Trilogy

That two-hour session at the back of the pet store had left Christian Grey feeling fresh and reinvigorated. Anastasia Stainless Steel had given him a proper seeing-to (even squeezed his butt glands). He felt marvelous. He straightened his favorite tie and smiled to himself; he couldn't wait to see her again and lick her face in gratitude.

William Makepeace Thackeray: Vanity Fair

Becky's new fortune had opened many doors. Here she sat, ankles crossed, in the corner of Lady Percy's grand salon.

Taking seven sandwiches and fourteen madeleines, she was oblivious of her faux pas until she looked up from the cup of tea she was daintily lapping.

HENRY MILLER: TROPIC OF CANCER

Ashley had never done topless before. But as she lay back on the photographer's couch and looked into the lens, she realized that she could do this. Like Gypsy Rose Lee, she would give them what they wanted but with class! A strategically placed paw or feathered fan would convey modesty while her eyes… well, her eyes would say, 'Take me, I'm all yours.' And then she might let them tickle her tummy a little bit.

Ian Fleming: James Bond

Licky la Derriere luxuriated in the silky sheets of the presidential suite's bed. Monte Carlo hadn't disappointed and neither had James. She hoped he wouldn't notice her dog fart as he returned with the macchiatos and croissants.

STAR TREK

Spock knew there would only be one chance to extract the coordinates of the Andorian home planet from the dying fugitive before the worm hole collapsed. A Vulcan mind-meld was his only recourse.

"Your mind to my mind... your thoughts to my thoughts..."

"Good grief, Dog! Get your paws off my face!"

Fiction Genre: Historical Romance

Samantha sunk into the silky pillows and looked over at him, boldly appraising his muscular frame. It was dizzying to think of the previous evening and how she had ended up here, in the Count's bed. She wished she had thought to trim her beard and eyebrows but how could she have known the night that lay ahead of her?

J. R. R. Tolkien: The Lord of the Rings

Griffin looked up at Gandalf, disbelief spreading across his whiskered face.

"I'm an actual Elf?!"

"Yes, my Son. You were taken in by Hobbits as a youngling, under my guidance. Did you never question the mahoosiveness and pointiness of your ears?"

"No but I often wondered about my thexy lithp!"

"You are indeed the child of Arwen. Now Sauron has turned his eye on you, you must return to her."

"Thauron? Oh thit!"

Mary Shelley: Frankenstein

He was overcome with a wave of horror for his creation, and yet it had some kind of ghastly appeal. Certainly, he could have made the nose a little smaller and perhaps given it more brains and toned down the squeaky bark, but it was so devoted and affectionate and would follow him everywhere…which was actually quite annoying. Perhaps he needed to go back to the drawing board.

Robert Louis Stevenson: Treasure Island

"Have ye seen a seafaring man by the name of Scurvy Dog in these here parts? He owes me fifty sacks of gold doubloons."

"Arrr no! I mean nope! I have no idea who you're talking about...Old Chap!"

"He has a curly moustache, a pale blue 'kerchief and a big nose...There's somethin' awfully familiar about ye, lad."

"Not seen him, Matey…I mean, Mate!"

D. H. Lawrence: Lady Chatterley's Lover

As he moved ever closer, I noticed his hot breath as it turned into clouds of steam in the cold air of the stables. Somehow thrilled by the anticipation of the gamekeeper's whiskers and dirty nails on my skin, I trembled.

Leaning in, he closed his sooty lashes and I felt the shock of his cold wet nose on my neck.

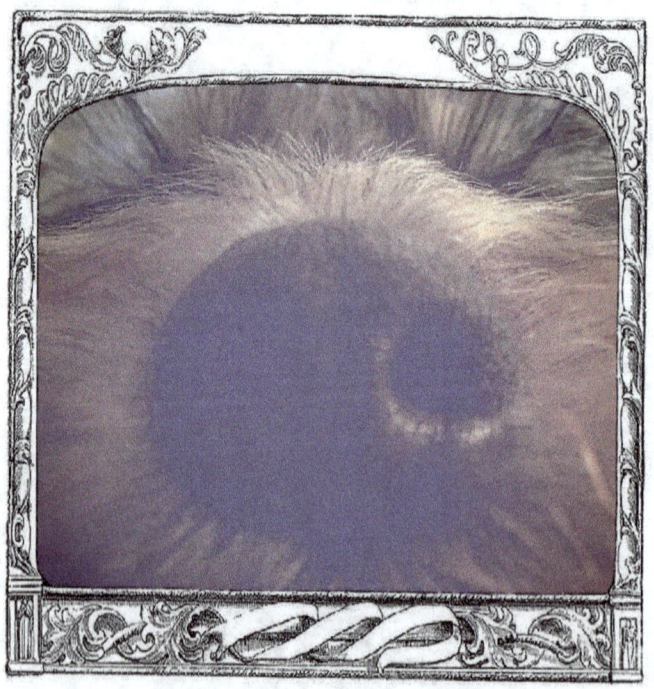

J.K. Rowling: Harry Potter

"Redactum Skullus!"

"Well, that worked; his head is tiny!"

"But now his bottom's too big."

"Oh. Try 'Redactum Rectum' "

"Okay…oh! That won't do at all!"

"Try 'Rectum Gigantium'."

"Ooh! That's a bit… that's very… You know what? We should get on; pretty sure I just heard the lunch bell!"

THE WOLF OF WALL STREET

Regrets? Max had no regrets. There would be others like him and Wall Street would always endure. He only felt a bit bad for old Mr Roberts who lost his entire life savings, house, car, wife and pension.

Movie Genre: Western

"Git yer hands up! I'm gonna hold up this here stagecoach and… you still there? And I'm gonna take all your… I can't actually see you, say something… ok, I'll be havin' yer jewelry, Ladies, and any… ooh! That a Bonio? That'll do nicely, Son! KEEP yer hands where I can see 'em! Are they up? Ok, super! Anyone seen ma horse?"

Acknowledgments

Thanks to Mike @thebottlewader for leaving the river to give me your excellent proof-reading services and Grant for your expert help and encouragement. Also, Shirley and Andrea and Lucky for modeling for me, and Moira, wherever you are. And once again, Almost Home Schnauzer Rescue and the late Joyce Pugh who found Max and Griffin for us.

Lizzie Nelson is a British artist and author living in the Chicago suburbs with her dogs. Oh! And husband and daughter.

She is the author and illustrator of **Fair to Piddling: A Journey Through Midlife in Humorous Verse** and writes about midlife under Fair to Middling on social media. She is also a frequent contributor to **Menopause Life** magazine. But her most inspired work is all the waffling she does about her rescue pups, Max and Griffin. Find them on Instagram and Facebook @thedogpoet.

She published the parody Jane Austen notebook **Writing with Jane** in 2021 and has illustrated children's books, most recently **Uncle Bill's Missing Tooth** by Grant S. Clark. Her first published piece was inclusion in the Twitter Anthology **VSS365**.

You can read more about her at fairtomiddling.weebly.com

If you enjoyed Doggy Biscuits, please consider leaving a review!

Available on Amazon and online booksellers worldwide:
Fair to Piddling: A Journey Through Midlife in Humorous Verse. Inspired by motherhood, early menopause, middle age and generally falling apart.

We Loved This!!!
Witty, funny & thought provoking.
Mark Adderley and Nadia Sawalha

I thoroughly enjoyed it, read it three times straight off. Sent it to my menopausal daughter but told her I wanted it back!
Beryl Cross aged 90

Fantastic!! Absolutely Fantastic, laugh out loud on every page. You will find yourself singing, laughing and laughing some more. Light-hearted, highly recommend.
The Menopause Queen

Closing Thoughts

When they ask,
'How did she go?'
They will say,
'Tragically,
she tripped over Max as he followed her around the
house.'
Or,
'The dogs saw a squirrel and pulled her into a lamppost.'
Or,
'She froze to death while waiting for Max
to find the perfect place to poo.'
Or,
'She died of fright when Max pawed her in the middle of
the night.'
Or,
'She choked on her food when a cold nose touched her
under the table.'
Or,
'She caught myxomatosis and mange after the dogs
rolled in something horrible.'

Yes. That is what they will say.

www.ingramcontent.com/pod-product-compliance
Lightning Source LLC
Chambersburg PA
CBHW070711130626
46553CB00005B/1937